TO: Lee Carr &
Family

I wish you all the best
in the world good health,
continued success!

J.M. Rose

TO: Order books:
Tel. (707)448-2975

Roseburton1942@gmail.com

YES-ANYONE CAN!

*A Secret to Attract Success By
Using the Three Big C Principles*

ROSE P. BURTON, PHD

WESTBOW
PRESS®
A DIVISION OF THOMAS NELSON
& ZONDERVAN

The purpose of this book is to educate and entertain; it is not to serve as the ultimate guide to success or as a substitute for psychological services.

Scripture quotations marked NLT are taken from the New Living Translation of the Bible, copyright 1996, 2004, 2007 by Tyndale House and used with permission. All rights reserved.

Scripture quotations marked NKJV are taken from the New King James Version copyright 1982 by Thomas Nelson. Used by permission. All rights reserved.

The writings of Mother Teresa of Calcutta are used with the permission of the Mother Teresa Center, exclusive licensee throughout the world of the Missionaries of Charity for the works of Mother Teresa.

On March 23, 2015, Christianbookpreviews.com granted permission to reprint a part or whole review from its website; see chapter 5, quote by Ann Hibbard.

WestBow Press books may be ordered through booksellers or by contacting:

WestBow Press
A Division of Thomas Nelson & Zondervan
1663 Liberty Drive
Bloomington, IN 47403
www.westbowpress.com
1 (866) 928-1240

Because of the dynamic nature of the Internet, any web addresses or links contained in this book may have changed since publication and may no longer be valid. The views expressed in this work are solely those of the author and do not necessarily reflect the views of the publisher, and the publisher hereby disclaims any responsibility for them.

Any people depicted in stock imagery provided by Thinkstock are models, and such images are being used for illustrative purposes only. Certain stock imagery © Thinkstock.

ISBN: 978-1-5127-1159-2 (sc)
ISBN: 978-1-5127-1158-5 (e)
Library of Congress Control Number: 2015914576

Print information available on the last page.
WestBow Press rev. date: 10/16/2015

In memory of my husband, John Thomas Burton, who encouraged and inspired me to write this book. My parents; sisters; brothers; grandson Colin James; daughter Ruth; my nieces Fe, Socorro, and Mila Rosa; and my readers. Above all, to the Creator of all things, the Lord God Almighty.

CONTENTS

INTRODUCTION

The heavenly Creator created me
To become a Creator
Filled with Creativeness
Therefore, I can Create
anything constructive.
—Dr. Rose P. Burton

As a Mental health official I have encountered many clients who were unable to succeed in life because they disliked reading thick, complex books. Many of them, unfortunately, remain uninformed in many areas that could have helped them on their road to success. They were under the impression that thick books were boring and hard to understand, and they told me they found technical advice difficult to comprehend. As a result, I decided to write this book in simple, understandable language.

I found a need, and I joyfully filled it. I hope this book will motivate people in all areas of their lives. This book is spiritually based and governed by the law of the creative mind, so if we think right, we will do right.

I hope my sprinkling of seeds throughout this book will encourage readers to grow closer to God and grow in all areas of their lives as well.

—Dr. Rose P. Burton

ACKNOWLEDGMENTS

I have received so much help in producing this book. I'll start by thanking all who have contributed to it and for believing in me. I thank the WestBow Press teams in Indiana and Cebu City in the Philippines. Special recognition goes to my agents John Lineback and Jenn Seiler, from WestBow Press, who trusted and believed in me as a first-time writer.

I thank Dr. Jonathan St. Cyr, who wrote the beautiful foreword, and all my mentors who inspired and taught me the "do it now" principle. I was able to overcome inertia, which is the enemy of that principle.

A gigantic thank-you to all the authors who provided the quotations in this book; their quotes are so instrumental in conveying my ideas and thoughts.

I send a warm thank-you to my secretary, Katrina Ashley Hill, who faithfully served with me throughout the initial stages of writing my book.

My immense appreciation and heartfelt gratitude go to my first-phase editor and contributing writer, Eva Louise Taylor, who also handled the final preparation of my book and made it ready for publication. She typed the book and did formatting, editing, and research as well as writing contributions to enhance, clarify, and expand upon my writings and ideas.

I make special mention of the pastors and congregation of The Father's House, Vacaville, California, who share with me their love and fellowship every Sunday morning. Their thoughtfulness and encouragement is a true treasure in my life.

My final words go to three wonderful people—my father, my mother, and most of all, my loving husband, John. I hope they can see me now.

FOREWORD

Dr. Rose Burton had a dream, vision, purpose, and mission. She created and patented the Rosie Turban for cancer patients. Due to that accomplishment, she was invited to the White House and awarded a Congressional Medal of Distinction in December 2006 (please see chapter 20, "A Goal Reach"). This award stated that Dr. Burton had been selected based on her unyielding support for the Republican Party and for outstanding leadership in business and contributions to the local economy.

When people ask Dr. Burton how she did it, her answer is, "I had a goal, I focused on what I wanted, I knew my direction, and my dreams were too big to be denied. I reached my goal!"

She hopes her readers will awaken their dreams, visions, purposes, and missions. She invites them to experience a higher level of thinking and find the road maps they have been seeking to make their hearts' desires come true.

Dr. Burton believes and will assure you that ordinary people can accomplish extraordinary things. Their dreams and ideas are needed in this world so others can follow.

Please let Dr. Rose Burton be your mentor in following your heart's desire.

—Dr. Jonathan St. Cyr, MD
Surgeon, Pilot, and Medical Advisor for
Continental Air Lines

Dr. Burton is a perfect example of what anyone can accomplish with faith, belief, positive attitudes, and a loving heart. I am in awe of what she has accomplished in her life. She came to the United States and succeeded, an enormous feat. She possesses an abundance of imagination, enthusiasm, creativity, and excitement for life and humanity.

She is a true blessing in my life. Readers will be encouraged and benefit greatly by reading her inspirational, informative, and straightforward book.

—Eva Louise Taylor
First-Phase Editor and Contributing Writer

CHAPTER 1

Getting Started

The fact that you are reading this book leads me to imagine many things about you. I'm guessing the title *Yes—Anyone Can!* caught your eye because you want to achieve goals in life. But perhaps you have already tried and failed, or your results weren't as good as you would have liked them to be, or you think you're too old and life has passed you by.

You may be thinking, *Others have succeeded, so why not me?* Maybe you think you're not good enough or smart enough or that you don't have the right background or education. Well, you are good enough and have the ability to accomplish anything if you really want it badly enough. In this book, you will learn to think more highly of yourself and gain skills, techniques, and tips to be happy and successful. You will also learn the Three Big C Principles.

Through our heavenly Creator, you can become a creator who gains creativeness and is thereby able to create whatever you want. This is all possible by taking some simple steps to acquire these principles.

I can attest to this because I have gained much through trial and error, positive attitude, determination, and the help of our God. All my efforts to achieve my goals were difficult because I was a foreigner to the United States adjusting to a new environment. However, with the help of my husband, I was able to understand and adapt to the American culture. I knew if I was going to live in the United States, I would have to do some adapting.

It was a little strange at first, but in time, I became comfortable in my new country and fell in love with it. While negotiating my way through this season of life, I grew personally a great deal. I was determined not to let anything get the best of me, and I kept my positive attitude with everything I encountered. The journey was very enlightening and liberating.

If I can do it, you can too! The chapters ahead will let you know how I found success in many areas. I have been very blessed with success and want to share all I have learned with you.

Keep in mind that our successes are not based just on the final products or accomplishments of our goals. Our successes come from many elements, foremost from within us. Being kind, honest, and loving individuals makes a huge difference. However, we must learn to love ourselves before we can show our love to others. How many times have you heard that? But it's true. One of the benefits of loving yourself is that you gain high self-esteem and are therefore more likely to treat others with kindness and respect.

What we put out there will come back to bite us or bless us. I prefer the blessing. Treat others as you would like to be treated—that's another saying with the ring of truth.

If we want to be treated with kindness, we must treat others kindly. Remember this and practice it with everyone who crosses your path because it will pay off in more ways than you can imagine. You can be remembered as kind, friendly, and helpful, or rude, hostile, and mean. Most of us want to be remembered the pleasant way, don't we?

Success doesn't happen overnight. There are many steps involved, and they start with baby steps. The mistake many of us make is trying to skip these initial steps or at least as many as we think we can to speed up the process. That rarely works; we must learn to crawl before we can walk (well, in most cases). We must go through infancy, early childhood, later childhood, and adolescence before becoming an adult—those are the steps we all have to take to maturity, and most things in life require steps to reach. This is actually a very good thing as we acquire more skills along the way and become more knowledgeable.

What is success? It's the feeling of happiness after accomplishing something that required enormous effort. It's the accomplishment of dreams and goals. Some measure success in terms of wealth, respect, and perhaps fame, but consider the Bible's recipe for success.

> Observe the requirements of the Lord your God and follow all His ways. Keep each of the laws, commands, regulations, and stipulations written in the law of Moses so that you will be successful in all you do and wherever you go. (1 Kings 2:3 NLT)

Following God's Commandments has played a major role in my success.

There are a million and one books out there that will offer you guidelines for success, but keep in mind that the most complicated solutions are not necessarily more effective than others. Keep it simple; you'll need to make hundreds of small decisions, you'll need to take hundreds of small steps to achieve success. While you're taking those steps, focus on honesty, simplicity, love, and kindness; that will make reaching your goals much easier and more joyful.

We all have reasons for wanting success. Each of us defines success in different ways. Some of us want financial freedom, some of us want to make names for ourselves, and some of us just want to feel a sense of accomplishment. Whatever your reason, get ready to discover how you too can become successful!

CHAPTER 2

Love and Kindness

I consider kindness a spiritual gift that is an essential sign of faith and a primary practice of Christian tradition. In chapter 1, I mentioned the importance of loving yourself so you can love others and show them kindness and generosity. Loving yourself and others creates peace and happiness within; consider it a step along your journey.

I consider peace and happiness to be by-products of love. God created us to love first Him and then one another. So by loving ourselves and others, we bring about happiness and follow God's rule. Can you imagine living in a world with absolutely no love?

The loving relationship we should have with ourselves is second in importance only to the loving relationship we should have with God. Loving yourself means accepting yourself as you are and learning to be okay with the things you cannot change. It means having self-respect and a positive self-image. It means having a humble, healthy regard for yourself and realizing your worth as a human being.

We can all find things about ourselves we don't like; we're our own worst critics in that way. We tend to focus on our negatives rather than on our positives. In more cases than not, others don't even notice what we've fixated on. Does that mean it's all in our heads? Not necessarily, but it does mean the significance we have placed on it is not necessarily of importance to others.

Make a habit of reminding yourself that no one is perfect. We are all unique and have special gifts, talents, and abilities we can and should share with the world. Yes, we all have our weaknesses as well, but by using our abilities and internal resources, we can improve ourselves. Once we discover our talents and our weaknesses, it's our responsibility to develop the talents and overcome our weaknesses to live the best lives we can.

Many of us wait for the approval from others instead of accepting and approving ourselves. We all want to be the best people we can be; that will help us succeed in all we do.

So how do you learn to love yourself? By devoting time and effort to your personal growth and development. By putting energy into becoming the best person you can be. Keep in mind that you're not superhuman; you need to achieve balance in your life. No matter your conditions and the obstacles you run into, you have the potential and spiritual capability to rise above them and go forward.

As you grow and learn to love yourself, you will find yourself wanting more balance in your life physically, mentally, and emotionally. By doing so, you will generate feelings of self-worth and accomplishment.

You will find yourself eating better, wanting to exercise, wanting new and different things, and giving yourself the proper amount of rest. And please, don't forget to take care of your precious spirit. Give yourself time to meditate, dream, and pray. This will help rejuvenate you, which in turn will help you deal with daily challenges.

Loving yourself takes practice, practice, and practice, but the result is a happier, healthier you! Take advantage of all your gifts and talents and become the true you. You are a special individual with unique qualities; God designed you that way, so how can you possibly be anything but special?

Love Yourself—Be Yourself

When you love, you automatically show kindness, which is part of your loving nature. You may be wondering, *What in the world does love and kindness have to do with achieving success?* Trust me; as you read this book, you will learn the link between kindness and success.

Most of us define *kindness* as giving of ourselves in ways that help others; showing them respect, love, thoughtfulness, and empathy; and being responsive to their needs. How does the act of kindness make you feel? Try to remember a time when you bought something for yourself you wanted. How did that make you feel? You were probably glad you bought it, but did it really make you happy? Now, think about a time when you bought a gift for someone, perhaps something you knew that person wanted. How did that make you feel? I bet you felt happier to have surprised that person than you did treating yourself to something. Do you remember that person's response? Did he or she smile, laugh, and express gratitude? You'll never go wrong by showing others kindness.

How can you develop the habit of being kind? That's simple. Every morning, ask God to show you someone who needs your kindness. He knows far better than we do who needs what, so I always rely on Him. In time, you'll be surprised at whom He puts in your path who are in need of a little kindness. Sometimes, it's as simple as smiling at someone; maybe that's all that person needed to brighten his or her day. Maybe you can show kindness with a simple please or thank you. It can take so little to show kindness to others. A genuine smile is a way of connecting with people, and friendships are often born from such simple gestures. We can all use more friends, right?

> *Be the living expression of*
> *God's kindness: kindness in*
> *your face, kindness in your*
> *eyes, and kindness in your*
> *smile.*
> —Mother Teresa[1]

As a volunteer greeter in my church, I have the opportunity and the pleasure to greet everyone with kindness and a big smile on Sunday mornings. One Sunday morning, I was greeting people at church as usual, and much to my surprise up walked Kenny and Donna, friends from

---

[1]   Mother Teresa, "Mother Teresa of Calcutta Center," n.d., at www.motherteresa.org/layout.html, accessed February 19, 2015.

church. They gave me a beautiful plant and a card. It was my birthday, and they had remembered that. Their kind gesture made my day. *Remembered* is the key word here; we all know being remembered means so much. Kenny and Donna had thought enough of me to remember it was my birthday; they hadn't forgotten that. That told me they thought enough of me to take precious time away from their busy lives to buy me a beautiful plant and write me a delightful note. That's a wonderful example of kindness!

I got permission from Kenny and Donna to present their card as evidence of their kindness.

> *Kindness is a combination of harmony and love. When properly used it is magnetic in nature. A wealth of health money cannot buy.*
> **—Dr. Rose Burton,** author of *Yes—Anyone Can!*

Habitually smiling and showing kindness will help us become more mindful of others and progressively change our attitudes. As we practice the art of kindness, our attitudes become more positive, and we automatically look at the brighter side of life, which is positive thinking. Possessing a positive attitude will help us immensely in all areas of life. A positive attitude is essential for success in everything we do. Consider the major changes we can undergo by simply showing kindness. It is almost magical how our personalities will change for the better when we give of ourselves to others.

You can practice and thus get better at praising people, making eye contact, and giving hugs, all of which are ways to make others feel important. Give these approaches a try and you will find much reward.

> *The benefits of humor and a nice smile to you and me extend far greater profit. You will also have the privilege of feeling better yourself and making others happy as well.*
> —Dr. Richard Carlson[2]

It takes time to develop a habit of kindness, but it will be well worth your efforts. Kindness brings about happiness, and we can all use more of that, right?

Realize and believe that we all can be kind and have a positive attitude; that ability comes from within. Once we become aware of this ability, we should go for it! We'll never be sorry.

I challenge you to smile at everyone you pass today. Tell them all, "Have a wonderful day," or ask them, "Isn't it a beautiful day?" Taking time to smile and speak to others

---

2   Dr. Richard Carlson, *Don't Worry, Make Money: Spiritual and Practical Ways to Create Abundance and More Fun in Your Life* (New York: Hyperson, 1997), 148.

makes them feel valued and puts smiles on their faces. What if your act of kindness helped someone chase suicidal thoughts out of his or her mind? What if your smile brought hope to a person feeling all alone? We have no idea what other people are thinking, going through, or needing, but just maybe, a simple smile and act of kindness might help change their days for the better. We can all benefit from getting outside ourselves and thinking more of others.

Step: Learn to be loving and kind.

Tip: Practice the principles of loving yourself and kindness, and surround yourself with people who live their lives according to these principles. Residing in an environment of love and kindness supports your steps forward.

CHAPTER 3

Enthusiasm Can Create Reality

Enthusiasm is such an important part of success that I hope you will wrap your head around the concept. It's one of the steps I mentioned earlier that is vitally important to your happiness, motivation, and success. It has such control, influence, and authority over your vast abilities. It's highly important and so exciting! It can enable you to create good habits and generate a wave of energy in you. Did you know you can actually create this powerful form of energy?

This energy is one that travels through the entire nervous system to create thoughts and feelings to

ultimate action. Above all else it also stimulates the entire nervous system.
—Iyanla Vanzant[3]

Let's consider the fundamentals of enthusiasm, which can create reality—authenticity, truth, and actuality—life itself. In his book *Enthusiasm Makes the Difference*, Dr. Norman Vincent Peale noted, "The word enthusiasm from the Greek 'en theos,' means God in you or full of God."[4] This definition is a simple but powerful statement. If God is in us, we can overcome all impossibilities and adversities. Thereby, to be inspired by God is enthusiasm. How encouraging is that?

Enthusiasm is a strong feeling we get when we're involved in something like a first solo flight; the feelings of excitement, fear, and joy at the same time increase our enthusiasm. We can experience enthusiasm when we encourage others. Enthusiasm is

---

[3]   Iyanla Vanzant, *The Spirit of a Man: A Vision of Transformation for Black Men and the Women Who Love Them* (San Francisco: HarperOne, 1997), 185.

[4]   Dr. Norman Vincent Peale, *Enthusiasm Makes the Difference* (New York: Touchstone, 2003), 129.

an eagerness or curiosity that can result in action. Sir Edward Appleton said, "The secret of his amazing discoveries is enthusiasm," and "rates enthusiasm even above professionals."[5]

Emerson said, "I believe that enthusiasm is the 'spice of life'" and "Nothing great was ever achieved without enthusiasm."[6]

If this powerful energy is in us, we can translate our thoughts and feelings into action. You and I are energy! We can express ourselves and become self-actualized individuals who create our own success. Yes, anyone can!

I remember taking my first flight. Some people would consider that a scary experience, but I passed that test with flying colors, and it included a successful landing. My success was due to my consciousness being powered by incredible energy—enthusiasm—my driving force. Without this powerful energy, it would have been impossible for me to complete this

---

[5]   Peale, *Enthusiasm*, 4.
[6]   Peale, *Enthusiasm*, 12.

extraordinary task with such ease and success.

Our enthusiasm can be so great that we will act without thought; it's a driving force that can take control of us and cause us to lose ourselves in what we do. Just think; we human beings can generate such power! Pretty incredible, huh? Enthusiasm can infuse our cells with wonderful, exuberant energy and cause our personalities to explode with creativity. I told you it was exciting!

Here's how I suggest you generate enthusiasm for whatever you do, and this holds true for everyone in spite of our different personalities. Personality is important; it's part of our souls, our very beings as I mentioned previously. Enthusiasm comes from the path in our human consciousness. Enthusiasm is the result of harmonious relations between our physical and mental attributes. If we are working with a "glass half full" positive attitude and a loving nature, the results of our enthusiasm will naturally be of high quality. If we're working with a negative attitude and hostile nature, our results will be poor.

We have a choice in the matter. Whatever we want to do will probably involve others at some point or another. Our enthusiasm will make us attractive in all kinds of relationships, personal as well as professional. People love spending time with enthusiastic people because that attribute is contagious.

Here are a few guidelines you can follow to generate enthusiasm.

1. Get motivated by surrounding yourself with enthusiastic people, and spend as much time as you can with them; their enthusiasm will rub off on you and get you going. And you'll have fun! Share with them whatever you're working on or want to do. They will probably have some great, enthusiastic ideas for you.

2. When you wake up each morning, sing this little jingle: "It's a new day, I'm alive, and I am enthusiastic!" If you don't like that, make up one of your

own and sing it. Singing will get you motivated and make you enthusiastic.

3. Make some time just for yourself. Get out into the fresh air, take a walk, ride a bike, kick a ball in the park, or exercise. You'll feel better, and you may see or hear something while stopping to smell the roses that will enthuse you. Enthusiasm is a sun shining brightly inside you that eases your life and makes it much more enjoyable.

4. Listen to upbeat music, sing along, shout, do a cheer, whatever. Start laughing for no reason at all and listen to yourself. It's infectious and will make you laugh even more.

5. Start a new hobby; do something you have never done before or perhaps two or three somethings you've never done before. I bet you'll discover talents you never knew you had. You'll be amazed and enthusiastic!

6. Spend time thinking about what you truly would like to do. This is the most important tip; it can generate

great enthusiasm without exerting much effort. When you're doing what you like to do, enthusiasm will flow naturally. How great is that?

7. If you're having trouble mustering up enthusiasm, it could be because you're not yet knowledgeable enough about whatever you're trying to motivate yourself to do. It's easy to get stuck; everyone does from time to time. Try digging a little deeper by going to the library or online and research your subject. You'll find interesting stuff that will ignite your enthusiasm and give you the incentive to go forward. If you stay positive, enthusiasm will follow.

8. Remember how you feel when you're enthusiastic and act that way. Do what you do when you're enthusiastic. In time, your acting lessons will pay off and make you feel enthusiastic.

9. Staying enthusiastic requires a lot of energy, so get plenty of sleep and exercise to stay healthy.

10. Be on the alert for negative influences or voices. They can come from many directions and can drain your enthusiasm. Replace the negatives with positives.

11. Ask the Creator of all things to help you with enthusiasm. God has commanded us to do unto others as we would have them do unto us—the Golden Rule. Wanting others to be happy and helping them in any way we can creates a feeling of fulfilment and pleasure, which creates enthusiasm.

    Whatever you decide to do in life, if you take time to help others along the way, your path and load will be lighter. You will go farther faster by helping others first.

We aren't through yet. Here's another creative way to motivate enthusiasm, which can motivate others and solve problems. Consider this equation; it can help us remember the steps we can take to acquire results.

E and P plus T, W and C, S, and F = R

More simplified:
E&P = Energy & Power
T   = Thought
W&C = Wisdom & Courage
S   = Strategy
F   = Faith
R   = Results

I based this equation on what Dr. Peale stated in *Enthusiasm Makes the Difference*: "When we claim for enthusiasm the power to work miracles in solving problems we are actually saying that God Himself in you supplies the wisdom, courage, strategy and faith necessary to deal successfully with all difficulties."[7] We need only to discover how to apply enthusiasm effectively when we're pondering our problems.

Positive thinking is not an option; it's a necessity and will help us be more creative in solving our challenges. I encourage us

---

[7]   Peale, *Enthusiasm*, 129.

all to continually tell ourselves, *I'm going to be successful.* In time, we will begin to believe it, see it, feel it, and act on it. These expectations will push us forward with enthusiastic eagerness!

> *Enthusiasm can release powerful forces and get them working for you.*
> —Norman Vincent Peale[8]

I had my share of struggles and obstacles with writing this book. It was difficult and time consuming to research facts and evidence that went into it, but we all know there's no gain without pain. Fortunately, my enthusiasm created the motivation I needed to complete my book.

My training in the mental health field taught me that the chief duty of human beings is to endure life. How depressing is that? Who wants to just endure life? There's a much better way to think about life—we should concern ourselves with mastering it. "Don't endure—master!" That has a ring to it, don't you think? It's a sound philosophy,

---

[8]   Ibid., 130.

an important and effective way to get on top of our daily problems. We should do what we need to do to master our lives and fill them with joy, happiness, and enthusiasm.

I'm grateful that I follow Dr. Peale's definition of enthusiasm; it's been a huge benefit for me and can be for you as well. Forming the habit of enthusiasm changed my personal life and can change yours as well from good to better to victorious.

Step: Develop your ability to be enthusiastic.

Tip: Enthusiasm makes your communication with others much more significant because when you feel enthusiastic, that feeling emanates through your body language and voice, and that allows you to send a much more powerful message. The more you practice being enthusiastic, the easier it becomes to be enthusiastic.

CHAPTER 4

Happiness Is a Choice

What exactly is happiness? It's a state of mental and emotional well-being. It's a feeling that ranges from satisfied to joyful and ecstatic. Some consider happiness a matter of wealth, good fortune, and prosperity.

While these statements are true, experts claim that happiness is temporary. We tend to think that happiness comes from getting something we don't have but want rather than recognizing and appreciating what we have. We often think materialistically; we think that the more we acquire, the happier we'll be. Unfortunately, we're never satisfied; the more we get, the more we want. Happiness isn't a result of getting what we want; it's a state of mind no matter our circumstances. To be happy, we must think happy, as we control our thoughts and emotions. Happiness motivates us to believe in ourselves, which empowers a more satisfying life. When we believe in ourselves, we generate energy that enables us to accomplish what we never thought possible. So think happy and think positive.

Can You Make Yourself Lastingly Happier?
  —Dr. Martin E. P. Seligman[9]

Be optimistic; look for the good in everything, including your circumstances. The negative might be more visual, but if you look hard enough, you'll spot the good.

Dr. Martin Seligman, the father of positive psychology, formulated an equation, his happiness formula, H = S plus C plus V, in which H refers to Enduring Happiness, which equals Set Point (S) plus

---

9   Dr. Martin E. P. Seligman, *Authentic Happiness: Using the New Positive Psychology to Realize Your Potential for Lasting Fulfillment* (New York: Atria Books, 2004), 44–45.

Circumstances (C) plus Factors under your Voluntary control (V).

Simplified Version:
H = Enduring **Happiness**
= **S** Your genetic **Set point**
+ **C** Intervening **Circumstances**
+ **V** Factors under your **Voluntary** control.

This formula gives us hope that we can attain higher levels of happiness regardless of our genetic predisposition. Even when negative emotions present themselves, we still have the ability to increase our happiness.

So happiness is attainable, but the question is, how do we attain it and—very important—keep it? We don't have to look far; just as with enthusiasm, each of us has the innate ability to achieve happiness. God didn't create us with sad hearts; He created us with happy hearts.

It boils down to choice. Some days are better than others, so we need to work on being optimistic and maintaining positive, committed intentions. We will help ourselves become successful and happy by making conscious decisions to take on the right attitudes and behaviors. Each day, we can choose to make finding happiness our priority; we can take advantage of all our circumstances and opportunities throughout the day. With practice, we can become more aware of our circumstances and the opportunities that come our way.

Sometimes, finding happiness requires us to look at our lives through a magnifying glass. We can find that our beliefs, values, emotions, and relationships need a little tweaking. And relationships are big! We all need people in our lives to add to our happiness. We need good friends as well as our families; we must place ourselves in happy environments populated by happy people. By following these principles, our personal growth will make us happier and more satisfied. Life is short, so we should live it to the fullest and enjoy every moment. We can do so by choosing to be joyful and happy.

The following are what I consider thought-provoking quotes that can increase our happiness and sense of well-being. Print them out and tape them to your bathroom mirror or refrigerator so you can read them daily. This will soon become a wonderful habit and a choice so that no matter your daily challenges, you can find joy and happiness. Look around. God has surrounded us with joy in everything; we just have to develop the courage and inspiration to recognize that.

Be hopeful for tomorrow
has never happened.
—Dr. Robert Schuller in *Happiness*
Is by A. R. Bernard[10]

Happiness and Enthusiasm are
Traveling Companions.[11]

Step: Find happiness.

---

[10]   A. R. Bernard, *Happiness Is … Simple Steps to a Life of Joy* (New York: Touchstone, 2011), 72.

[11]   Bernard, *Happiness Is*, 160.

Tip: If you make finding joy and happiness your priority, you'll find that everything in your life will flow much easier. Stopping and smelling the roses means taking time daily to enjoy and be happy. So do it! Learn to enjoy your life.

CHAPTER 5

Do Friends Play a Role in Our Success?

What is a friend? Most of us have acquaintances, but do we have true friends? We all need friends—two, three, or a dozen. Although acquaintances are nice, they don't have the same feelings for us as our true friends do.

I read an excerpt from Ann Hibbard's *Treasured Friends—Finding and Keeping True Friendships*. The excerpt was so interesting, exciting, and motivational that I put it on my list of books to read. Hibbard believes that to have and maintain good friendships, we must be what we wish for in a friend. Friends need to listen to one another with compassion and respect and be supportive and honest in all circumstances.

True friends encircle us with the support that we need. Without this circle of friendship, we easily fall prey to discouragement, depression, fear, and self-centeredness. When we are functioning as God designed us, our lives knit together in interlocking circles of trust.
—Ann Hibbard[12]

I encourage my mental health clients to spend time with their close friends and make new friends. It's not healthy to spend all our time alone; we need each other for companionship and fellowship.

Wishing to be friends is quick work, but friendship is a slow ripening fruit.

---

[12] Ann Hibbard, "Treasured Friends: Finding and Keeping True Friendships," www.christianbookpreviews. com/christian-book-excerpt.php?isbn=0800787137, accessed February 19, 2015.

Aristotle[13]

Here's my idea of the type of friend you want.

- A friend who listens to you without passing judgment or interrupting you with what he or she might do or think.
- A friend you can trust. Without trust, there can be no true friendship.
- A friend willing to pray with and for you. There's no better way to grow your friendship than sharing God with your friend.
- A friend to help and support you; one who is loyal and willing to set aside his or her concerns when you're in need.
- A friend who accepts you as you are, someone you feel totally comfortable around. That doesn't mean your friends will always approve of what you do or say; it means they still love you no matter what and will offer

---

[13]   Aristotle; died 322 BC.

loving counsel when you're moving in the wrong direction.

- A friend with whom you can share your joys and sorrows. He or she will be by your side on good and bad days alike.
- A friend who will love and respect your wishes even if he or she is not in agreement with you.
- A friend to hope and dream with you and inspire you to keep going no matter the circumstances. Such a friend will help you climb your mountains and capture your dreams.
- A friend to challenge you to be the best you can be and succeed at your heart's desires.

You may not find all these attributes in one person, but if you're covered by many friends, you'll be blessed. True friends will be there for you and help you in many ways to achieve and succeed in life. They will play important roles in your achieving success.

*The glory of friendship is not the
outstretched hand, nor the kindly
smile, nor the joy of companionship;
it is the spiritual inspiration that
comes to one when you discover that
someone else believes in you and is
willing to trust you with a friendship.*
—Ralph Waldo Emerson[14]

A true friend is a gift from God, who knows exactly what we need and when we need it. Having a relationship with God allows us to see and hear with our hearts. He often uses people and circumstances to get our attention so He can direct our paths.

If you want true friends, ask God. He will send you beautiful people with self-sacrificing hearts and godlike attitudes.

*My help comes from the Lord, who
made the heavens and the earth!*

---

14   Ralph Waldo Emerson (1803–1882).

I am holding you by your right hand—I, the Lord your God. And I say to you. "Do not be afraid. I am here to help you."

God has made everything beautiful for its own time. He has planted eternity in the human heart, but even so, people cannot see the whole scope of God's work from beginning to end.
—Psalm 121:2; Isaiah 41:13; Ecclesiastes 3:11 NLT

Friends play a role in our happiness and success, so take time to reach out and befriend others and watch how that can change their lives and yours for the better. I'm blessed to be a greeter in my church; every Sunday, I can touch the lives of others and befriend them. I view friendships as sacred relationships of the highest honor that are never defined by time or space; they are the earthly manifestation of divine love and one of life's richest blessings designed by our God.

Step: Make true friends.

Tip: Make true friends who can come alongside you for fellowship and support; that will aid your success. Calling upon God in your time of need will also help you achieve success.

CHAPTER 6

Work Can Be Fun

Every time I go to work as a Mental health official, I put on an attitude of happiness so I can create an environment of harmony for my clients and myself. This lets me enjoy my work and be more productive. This process is called programming the mind.

You can program your mind by mentally focusing on your thoughts, attitudes, and ideas—the way you think and function. If you want to reprogram your mind, that tells me you're not happy with the way you've been thinking and operating. Maybe your operating portion is okay and you just need to reprogram your thinking. You can reprogram any part of your mind, and that

41

will help you achieve success. Sound good so far?

I'm sure you've heard, "What the mind can conceive and believe, it can achieve,"[15] and "As a man thinketh in his heart, so is he" (Proverbs 23:7 NKJV), and other quotes that make the same point. We've all been programmed in some fashion. How many TV commercial ditties and songs have you memorized because you've heard them repeatedly? Companies want you to remember their jingles so you'll remember the companies when you shop. Advertisements are programming. If companies can program our minds, we can too!

Telling your inner self that you're just playing and enjoying it when you work can change your attitude about your job. It will soon not feel like a job; it will be an enjoyable event every day. Your environment will change from dull and dreary to joyful and happy. Once that transformation takes place, you'll look forward to going to work

---

[15] Kimbro and Hill, *Think and Grow Rich*, 37.

and be more enthusiastic, energetic, and productive when you're there. Your mind and body will be grateful.

It takes time to program your creative or subconscious mind, but if you're serious about it and spend some time each day repeating aloud your goals and wishes, you will program your mind just as TV commercials can.

This is a way to turn any job into a gratifying experience. Gardening is a good example. I love working in my garden for hours; I never tire of it. Instead, I get inspired because I asked for God's help in programing my mind to not think of it as work but as enjoyment. As a result, I look at my garden as an environment of harmony and beauty, and I love what I do.

It is not doing the thing we like to do,
but liking the thing we have to do,
that makes life blessed.
—Johann Wolfgang Von Goethe[16]

---

[16] Johann Wolfgang Von Goethe; died 1832.

I once interviewed a great leader of a large, well-known church. I asked him if leading a large group of people was hard. He said, "Oh no! Dr. Rose, I see it as just having fun with the guys." His was a mind programmed to enjoy!

God has the power to manifest our human desires. If we call upon Him and truly believe, accept, and expect His help, we can overcome almost any obstacle.

The Bible tells us, "Commit your work to the Lord, and then your plans will succeed" (Proverbs 16:3 NLT). We grow and work at our own pace; we are all different in personality, looks, abilities, and so on. We all, however, have one attribute in common, and that is our God. He gave us brains; if we use them properly, we can make our way and make a difference for ourselves as well as for humanity.

Experts claim we have about 20 billion nerve cells in our brains and each is capable of transmitting electrical current between one thousand and a hundred thousand nearby nerve cells. Each transmission represents a memory that can recombine with other memories to create new thoughts, ideas, and capabilities. Our ability to be creative is endless if we truly use the magnificent brains our Creator entrusted us with.

You're reading this book hoping to learn more about how you can succeed with your dreams and ideas. You're capable of doing anything you want in life. I have set goals, worked through struggles, persevered, and accomplished great results, and you can too! Have faith, believe, be positive and determined, have fun, and use your magnificent brain.

I hope my book will motivate you to recognize the vast abilities within yourself.

Step: Program your mind.

Tip: Review your thought patterns and see if they need altering.

CHAPTER 7

Spiritual Abundance

Can anyone claim an abundant life and success? Is it true all that's required is setting goals, making plans, and being determined to receive spiritual abundance? Yes. Sounds simple, doesn't it? Well, it is simple, but it requires taking steps, and we need a belief system to get there. I don't want to scare anyone; I want everyone to know he or she can take one step at a time and it will all come together. Abundance doesn't happen all at once just because we have asked for it. We must specifically prepare and be ready to accept it.

To achieve abundance in life, we must recognize, be knowledgeable of, and have faith in the nature of the unseen part of our universe and the way it works. Some call the "unseen" part of our universe faith and others call it intelligence, but wise men and philosophers call it the mind of God. Faith is key to receiving. We must have faith to bring things from the unseen realm of the spirit world into the seen realm, earth.

What is Faith? It is the confident assurance that what we hope for is going to happen. It is the evidence of things we cannot yet see.
—Hebrews 11:1 (NLT)

God has given us powerful gifts—our incredibly creative minds, including our subconscious minds. We need only to discover how magnificent they are and use them properly. If we do, we will accomplish our hearts' desires. The Bible tells us, "All that the father has is mine" (John 16:15 NLT). So let's stop telling ourselves that gaining abundance is impossible and start doing what's necessary to achieve it.

If you want abundance, spend time in meditation and prayer and understand the Spirit that resides in you. Allow your spirit mind to be open to receiving spiritual abundance. The more you allow and receive, the more you can share with others, and sharing is an important aspect of receiving abundance.

It is also important to develop spiritual energy, which is unseen, cannot be destroyed, and resides in us. It's considered the foundation from which flow our deepest and most lasting purposes. Spiritual energy provides us mental energy, which is the foundation of physical energy. Physical energy lasts only so long; when we use it up, we become exhausted, and we need more of it. Fortunately, we can revive ourselves through rest, prayer, and meditation.

For I can do everything with the help of Christ who gives me the strength I need.
—Philippians 4:13 NLT

Another good habit to get into is saying, "In the name of Jesus," and then speaking your requests. This technique is ancient, and it works! You can and should affirm exactly what you're asking for. You could say in an affirmative manner, "I'm a child of God, and I attract success and abundance because of whom He made me." It doesn't have to be that exact affirmation; think about what you desire and craft your affirmation accordingly.

By training (mantras, affirmations, meditation, and prayer) and relying on your mind's creativity, you will continuously be conditioning your brain, growing in knowledge and understanding, and believing in spiritual energy.

You can use Philippians 4:13 (just above) as one of your affirmations to reach a higher level of abundant life. If you accept, expect, and believe abundance is already yours, you can receive it. Yes, anyone can!

Try fine-tuning your time with God and you'll soon realize He is your heavenly Father who wants with all His heart the best for you. He loves you unconditionally. Everything He sends our way has a purpose. Be thankful and filled with awe and appreciation, and always thank Him.

> *And God will generously provide*
> *all you need. Then you will always*
> *have everything you need and plenty*
> *left over to share with others.*
> —2 Corinthians 9:8 NLT

Step: Believe in spiritual abundance.

Tip: Our treasures come from the stream of ideas our Creator gives us, so we should cash in on these ideas and use them not only for our benefit but for the benefit of others as well. God will be proud!

CHAPTER 8

The Power of the Creative Mind

Mental power is an extremely useful tool we can use to achieve self-development and improve our visualization techniques. We can awaken our hidden talents by imagining a blueprint for success in all areas of our lives. By believing, accepting, and practicing the principles of the creative mind, we can learn to control our thoughts and use them for others' benefit as well as our own.

Researchers know that the images we project in our minds will help us create a "biology" of success. The mental power of the mind is mental imagery. Someone suffering from an illness can use mental imagery to get better. The mental imagery technique goes something like this. Imagine your body is healing itself. Visualize each step of the healing process. Do this repeatedly. Your perception will be enhanced due to your senses behaving under the influence and command of your creative mind. It's mind over matter, and yes, anyone can! Mental imagery can affect you physically, emotionally, and psychologically.

This process is a combination of mind and body. When our minds are stretched by new ideas, they will never regain their original dimensions because those who believe in their dreams create their destinies. They learn to solve their problems creatively and know they can make things happen.

Things don't just happen; we must make them happen by being open minded, consistent with our goals, determined about what we want, planning, and using our creative minds for visualization and imagery. Go for it!

Part of the process of mental imagery is thinking positively on a consistent basis; that will increase our mental energy.

Exercise and healthy eating habits are wise and beneficial. Oh, by the way, the way we think and believe plays a role in the process also.

Mother Teresa created one of the world's greatest charities out of her very modest but well-organized surroundings by using her very creative mind and visualizing the possibilities even with starting from so little. It worked!

We do this by utilizing our imagination process. Experts call this process "involution equals evolution"; we must use the "involution" process before we can experience the result, the evolution we desire. Our imaginations are limitless if we don't limit what goes into our imaginations. Imagination is the foundation of greatness. Try these "imaginative" exercises.

- Challenge yourself to envision what is not and yet what can be.
- Use your creative mind to imagine what you haven't seen in the material world.

What if you could make your everyday life exciting and full of joy? What if you could turn unwanted behaviors into productive habits? What if you could create the perfect conditions for your success? These what ifs can happen! That will take time and practice, as is the case with anything worth doing, but the rewards will never end. I like the sound of that!

As with most new adventures, steps come into play. I have what I call my ABCs of basic mental imagery. Being aware of these fundamentals can impact the quality of your mental imagery. If you work on developing each of these areas, you'll get more out of your imagery.

- **Mental Picture**: Think of yourself as a movie camera as you visualize so you will see your imagery from inside out.
- **Mental Switch**: Switch on your confidence button, the one that tells you, "I can do this!" You will then imagine yourself doing whatever you want to do.

- **Detailed Visualization of Event**: When you visualize, do so with color, sounds, thoughts, emotions, even the mental and physical sensations you would feel. The importance here is how clearly you see yourself doing the imaginary event. Believe it is really happening, and don't allow negative imagery into your visualization.

If you practice these fundamentals, you will start feeling you're actually in your visualization. When this happens, you will know you've succeeded in mental imagery. But always be realistic in your imagery. As you visualize your event, be sure to visualize it where it will actually take place. All details need to be as realistic as if it were truly happening.

The key to getting the most out of mental imagery is consistency. Set your goals, practice mental imagery with simple scenarios, and build up your ability before trying to achieve your primary objective. Find a private area, set a time limit, and practice these techniques two to four times a week. I know you'll start seeing results.

Have you noticed a common thread running through the preceding chapters? Everything we've covered starts from within us, and as we use these God-given abilities, they help us and flow into the outside world as well.

Step: Understand and use your creative mind.

Tip: As you imagine yourself performing in whatever your event is, your body should move along with the imagery. Many professionals do this and it helps immensely. It's worth a try!

CHAPTER 9

The Causes of Failure

Why are many people not successful while others enjoy all kinds of success? As a mental health official I get this question frequently from my clients. The answer is simple; it's due to the way people think. We can unknowingly feed our brains negative thoughts that our creative minds pick up. I use the term *creative mind* instead of *subconscious mind* because God gave us creative minds.

Below are some of the reasons people fail. They may open your eyes to some ways you may be unknowingly making mistakes and sabotaging your chances of success.

After you become aware of your faults, you can work on correcting them.

1. **Lack of well-defined life goals.** You must make a decision as to what you want to accomplish; how else could you progress?

2. **Lack of accurate choices**. Don't act on what you think you know, act on what you actually know—facts! Do your homework before making important decisions.

3. **Fears.** If fears of low income, criticism, poor health, envy, old age, and death have gripped you, try meditation, prayer, positive thinking, mind imagery, and so on, to escape them. Read books about entrepreneurs; many of them started with some of these fears.

4. **Lack of drive, desire, and motivation.** It's difficult to progress if you lack incentive.

5. **Lack of enthusiasm**. We talked about this extensively in chapter 3, but it's

so important that it belongs in this list. Review chapter 3 repeatedly.

6. **Lack of the right people in your life**. Choose to include trustworthy, caring, inspirational, intelligent, and successful people in your life no matter what you're trying to succeed at. They can be encouraging to you and vice versa.

7. **Poor money management**. If you don't manage your money well, you'll have a hard time getting ahead. Get in the habit of putting aside a percentage of your income. Being prepared for financial emergencies will help you feel safe.

8. **Lack of physical and mental health**. Proper nutrition and a positive attitude are extremely important. How can you accomplish anything if you're sick and depressed?

9. **Procrastination**. Many are waiting for the right person to come along to encourage them. Some are waiting for just the right time. If not now, then

when? You'll never succeed if you don't try, so start trying!

10. **Lack of persistence**. Once you start, you must continue. How will you ever know if you can be a success if you stop trying?

11. **Lack of decision-making abilities**. We have to make decisions if we want to succeed. The quicker we make decisions, the quicker we will see results. And if at first we don't succeed, we should try, try again. Try plan A; at least we will have started. We can always go to plan B. We must not let procrastination and indecision set us up for failure.

12. **Negative personality**. In most cases, other people play important roles in what we're trying to accomplish. If we want assistance and support from other people, we have to rid ourselves of all negative attitudes. Otherwise, we'll find it difficult to attain and retain the help of others. People don't like spending time with negative people, and if we are

negative, we won't have much hope of fulfilling our dreams.

13. **Stuck in a depressing job**. Find work that you like doing. If you like what you do, you'll be happier doing it and success will come.

14. **Not realizing that if there's no pain, there won't be any gain.** If you aren't willing to work hard, you stand little to no chance to achieve success.

15. **Multitasking.** Don't *s-t-r-e-t-c-h* yourself thin. Stick to one project at a time so you can concentrate on it. If you're juggling several balls, you'll more than likely drop some.

16. **Lack of self-control, willpower, and discipline**. You must be in control of yourself before you can control anything else. Self-discipline is hard to come by, but it's worth it.

17. **Inability to get along with others**. This is a major problem in our society. It's such a shame; it's caused people to lose their jobs and other good things in their lives. Hostile, unfriendly people are just not wanted

or tolerated. If you're hostile and unfriendly, seek help.

These aren't all the possible causes of failure, but these will make you stop and think. Do any of them sound familiar? If you follow the advice in this book, you'll be able to make the changes you need and be on the road to success. William Whewell said, "Every failure is a step to success."[17] This is so true because failure is never final; there's a solution to every problem, and as you work through your failures, you'll become more knowledgeable about solutions to them. You will have taken several more steps toward success.

Our greatest glory is not in never failing, but in rising every time we fall
—Confucius

The greatest people in history made mistakes and failed. Alexander Graham Bell, Thomas Edison, and many more failed

---

[17] William Whewell (1794–1866), an important and influential figure in nineteenth-century Britain.

thousands of times before they succeeded. You have the power in you to succeed, so don't give up until you achieve success. Using affirmations, prayers, and meditation along with discipline and consistency empowered me to discover tremendous power from within and how to use it.

Reading a list of causes of failure is pretty depressing, right? I don't want to leave you depressed; that's the opposite of what I want to do. Let's finish this chapter on a positive note. Here's my list of the steps involved in achieving success, much more fun than reading roadblocks to success.

- Know what you want.
- Develop a plan to achieve it.
- Be open; believe your dream will come true.
- Be consistent in your efforts.
- Employ creative thinking.
- Use your imagination.
- Develop self-discipline.
- Visualize your goal as though you've already achieved it.
- Don't procrastinate.

- Develop a positive mental attitude.

Feeling better? Those who are successes exercise the creative part of their brains and use it to their full benefit. They realize the importance of setting goals, showing kindness, being enthusiastic, having a positive attitude, nurturing friendships, seeking spiritual abundance, and engaging in mind imagery as we talked about in previous chapters. All these elements and steps can help us in the pursuit of success.

Another element of the mind is about having a grand vision. In his book *Think and Grow Rich—A Black Choice*, Dr. Dennis Kimbro described grand vision as a "surging dynamic that is invisible to all the world except the person who holds it responsible for every advance of mankind."[18]

This grand vision is a goal you can reach by using your creative mind that will eventually be released to the world. As a result, you will see many things around you

---

[18] Kimbro and Hill, *Think and Grow Rich: A Black Choice* (New York: Fawcet, 1991), 87.

that started with a grand vision. Here are some excellent examples.

- Skyscrapers—Someone must have thought building up instead of out would save space as well as adding structural flavor.
- Beautiful, expansive bridges—that connect people everywhere.
- A shuttle to outer space—I can almost feel these grand visionaries' creative minds ticking.

We admire things without realizing they started as grand visions in someone's creative mind; someone like you and me. Yes, anyone can!

Reaching our goals is possible; so many people have reached theirs. Accepting that we have God-given, creative minds with many abilities, believing in ourselves, anticipating, expecting, visualizing, meditating, and praying can help us overcome all our obstacles to success. We must rid ourselves of the causes of failure, all the negativity and fear, and begin thinking the way successful people do.

The Creator gave me a creative mind, and I've used it to the best of my ability. One of my successful adventures was inventing the Rosie Turban for my cancer patients. (You'll read about this in chapter 13.) A need presented itself to me, and with my creative mind, I was able to fill that need.

Don't waste the gifts God has granted you; rather, use them to the best of your ability, and as you do, remember to give God the glory.

Step: Figure out why you have been failing.

Tip: Remember, "Anything is possible if a person believes" (Mark 9:23 NLT).

CHAPTER 10

Using Your Law of Mind

Life is what we make it. If we've had bad luck in life, it's not because of misfortune but because of our limited belief in the power of the conscious mind. We often block blessings coming our way because we've programmed our minds to believe they'll never arrive.

We can't enjoy blessings and gifts until we remove our mental blocks and learn how to accept them. Once we learn the law of mind, we can pick and choose our destinies.

If you've been experiencing bad luck, the fault most probably is in your thinking process. You probably have been telling yourself to expect the worst. It's not good to think that way because the laws of the mind are naturally creative.

We must learn to use our creative minds correctly; otherwise, we may unknowingly be programming them to expect bad luck. We have to pay attention to the ideas and attitudes we're putting into our minds. We can eliminate bad luck by simply thinking positively. There's so much more to the concept of the law of the mind, a fascinating concept, but I don't have the time or space here to delve into it in depth.

Dr. Ernest Holmes, who wrote *This Thing Called You*, wrote, "The laws of mind can be made to control the physical body and the physical environment when they are rightly used, not through denying body or environment, but including them in a larger system."[19] We all have the power to choose our destinies and respond to our circumstances. So what role does chance and luck play in our lives? Life has all these facets, circumstances, and conditions, but we

---

[19]   Dr. Ernest Holmes, *This Thing Called You* (New York: BN Publishing, 2007), 18.

can choose positive or negative outcomes. I always choose positive. You have a choice; what will it be? Be careful of what you say or think; your mind will respond to that.

We can be empowered with renewed strength and courage by choosing a colorful direction to go positively forward! In so doing, all our endeavors and circumstances will be constructive because we can make positive choices and reject negative opinions. We must decide what we want and program our minds for it.

One great mind who inspired me to write this book is Muhammad Ali. This professional boxer said, "I am the greatest! I actually said that before I even knew that I would be famous. Don't tell me I can't do something, don't tell me it's impossible, don't tell me I'm not the greatest, I am the double greatest!"[20] Although this may seem arrogant, Ali was doing the right thing by programming his mind and speaking about the victory he was looking for. He was a fearless believer that anything was possible. He was among many

---

[20] Cynthia Kersey, *Unstoppable* (Naperville, IL: Sourcebooks, 1998), 127.

who chose persistence, perseverance, and discipline; he was unstoppable.

By motivating and affirming yourself daily, programing your mind that is, ideas will come alive. The great motivational speaker and author Earl Nightingale said, "Each of us has our own idea factory. Learn to expect the best of everything."[21] Get your creative juices moving, put on your thinking cap, and use your idea factory.

When I was working on my Rosie Turban invention, I immersed myself in creative thought and unlocked my hidden talent. I received a special vision on how to design and construct my invention. You too can convert your creative thinking and imagination into success. Creative intelligence is the source of all things.

Step: Learn to use the law of mind correctly.

Tip: Any thought or image placed in your subconscious develops into reality. Practice makes perfect; create your perfect life with your thoughts.

---

[21] Kimbro and Hill, *Think and Grow Rich*, 49.

CHAPTER 11

If You Believe You Can Do It, You Can!

What motivates an individual to accomplish something great when everyone is saying, "That's impossible!"? It's because of that individual's belief system. What we think and believe manifests itself; this is why positive belief systems are so important.

Your strong positive belief system will encourage you and produce success, whereas a weak, negative belief system will keep you down and hinder your ability to accomplish your goals. Developing a positive belief system will allow you unlimited potential.

Claude M. Bristol, author of *The Magic of Believing*, wrote, "I firmly believe that there is a factor, a power, a science which few people understand and use this force to overcome their difficulties and achieve outstanding success."[22] If our belief systems are strong, that works to our benefit and allows us to become champions in all areas of our lives.

Once you learn, grow, and become a champion, you will have the ability to influence others as well as yourself. You'll be able to teach others what you have learned; you'll share and thus pass on your knowledge.

When God calls on us to share our abundance, He means not only material things but knowledge as well. As we share our abundance, it becomes useful to all humanity and future generations. An example of this is my invention of the Rosie Turban for cancer patients. It's my greatest contribution to humanity, but I give all the glory to God. I'm so thankful for all my

---

22   Claude M. Bristol, *The Magic of Believing* (Chicago: Snowball Publishing, 2011), 1.

mentors who shared with me an enormous amount of knowledge, and through this book, I am able to share with you as well.

What do you think? do you believe in the power of the mind and a strong belief system? I hope that by the time you finish reading this book, you will believe and use your God-given capabilities to overcome your difficulties and with consistency, diligently pursue your goal of achieving outstanding success.

The curtain is open. The stage is yours. You have the power to make your life an award winning success. Step in the spot light and go for it.
—Dr. E. Carol Webster, psychologist and author[23]

Believe in yourself, and be ready to accept the blessings available to you. Seldom does true achievement come suddenly; it comes step by step. Procrastination often gets in

---

[23] Dr. E. Carol Webster, *Success Management: How to Get to the Top and Keep Your Sanity Once You Get There* (Florida: Privileged Communications, 1993), 2 of acknowledgements.

our way; it's the enemy of success. Don't put off to tomorrow what you can do today.

Have you ever paid attention to how successful people look and act? Most of them stand out in crowds. What is it about them that all notice? I believe they worked on and developed positive self-images through all the channels and steps we have been discussing; a balanced blend. They developed a positive attitude, programed their minds with what they wanted to accomplish, visualized from beginning to achievement, acted like winners, spoke like winners, dressed like winners, believed as winners believe, and anticipated the best results, just as winners do.

Your creative mind is capable of magnificent accomplishments! As you work on developing your self-image to include all the above, avoid negativity in thought and action. If negativity happens to slip in, immediately cast it out and continue with your positive mind-set. Yes, anyone can!

Expecting the best is a form of creative anticipation. This process stops us from constantly expecting failure. It's a "matter" of mind over matter, so go for the gusto. Think big, more than big, and realize your dreams.

Dr. William James, the father of psychology, wrote, "The greatest discovery of my generation is that human beings can alter their lives by altering their attitude of mind."[24] His words are true; if we want to achieve greatness, we must believe in and use our creative minds with all their magnificent abilities. If we truly use our minds to full capacity, our achievements will be limitless.

Once you comprehend and conquer the use of your creative mind to full capacity, your belief system will be so strong that you'll feel unstoppable! This is how I feel; nothing stops me from exploring many avenues. I wanted to become a pilot, and I discovered that flying was a way to explore and appreciate God's creation. I feel so privileged to fly high and look down on hills, mountains, streams, and rivers; God's natural beauty is breathtaking! I believe

---

[24] Dr. William James, known as the father of American psychology.

there truly is a maker of all the indescribable beauty our universe holds, and I believe that's God.

While I was taking flying lessons, my curiosity led me to do some research about astronauts. I was so enthralled with the sights that I was seeing from up in the air that I wanted to learn about astronauts' experience in outer space. I got hold of Dr. Nancy J. Currie, retired U.S. Army colonel. Here are a few of Dr. Currie's statements taken from *Life Messages: Inspiration for the Woman's Spirit*, by Josephine Carlton.

> I think flying in space gives you a unique perspective because I don't see how you could fly in space and not have pretty strong spiritual beliefs. Because when you look out the window, you don't see this world of chaos. You see this exceptionally beautiful world. Almost indescribable beauty.[25]

---

[25] Josephine Carlton, *Life Messages: Inspiration for the Woman's Spirit* (New Jersey: Andrews McMeel,

What I gained from the description of Dr. Currie's experience is the sense that our world has great order and symmetry and a presence or sense of a higher being who created all the wonder and beauty.

I wish we all could have this exceptional opportunity to see what Dr. Currie saw in outer space. I believe it would strengthened our belief in God and perhaps encourage nonbelievers.

Then God looked over all He had made, and He saw that it was excellent in every way. This all happened on the sixth day.
—Genesis 1:31 (NLT)

Step: Learn to control your thoughts and actions.

Tip: Our thoughts and actions are governed by cause and effect, the consequences of actions.

2002), 171.

CHAPTER 12

Never Forget Those Who Helped You Climb the Ladder

My mother told me, "Striving to climb the ladder of success is a state of mind." So how do we climb the ladder? Her belief was, "Never wait for the perfect opportunity because it may never come along; jump right in and get things started. Whether it's for you or helping someone else, time waits for no one."

You will never win if you never begin.
—Dr. Robert Schuller[26]

---

26   Dr. Robert Schuller, *Power Thoughts: Achieve Your True Potential through Power Thinking* (New York: Harpercollins, 1993), 236.

On your journey to success, you'll encounter many people who will influence you. Perhaps a mentor, a financial advisor, an encouraging pastor, a teacher, a supportive friend, or Mom, who always has your best interests at heart—all will contribute in some fashion. Some contributions may be minute while others will be very noticeable. All contributions, no matter their size, are of great importance in shaping your journey to success. You should appreciate the help you have received and sincerely thank and praise everyone who has helped you.

Reflect on all the people who have helped you get to where you are, including those who made you laugh when you were down, who made you strong when you were at your weakest point, and all those who encouraged you to never give up.

Trouble knocked on the door, but hearing laughter, hurried away.
—Benjamin Franklin[27]

---

27 Patsy Clairmont et al., *Laughter is the Spice of Life* (Tennessee: W Publishing, 2004), 176.

As success comes to you, never forget where you started. Success often has a way of changing who we really are, and we can soon forget how and why we got there. Don't lose sight of what's truly important in your life—love, family, and friends. Remain humble, and never forget the people who helped you. Treating others with love and respect is always the right thing to do.

Just as you have received and appreciate help, make a point of helping others as much as you can. Help comes in different ways. If you cannot afford to financially help someone in need, give of yourself in another way. Perhaps you can offer suggestions from what you have learned on your journey that perhaps could save someone else a lot of time and grief.

> *When we give of ourselves to help others it brings enrichment and new meaning into our lives.*
> Dr. Rose Burton, author of
> *Yes—Anyone Can!*

I have done just that all my life. I have encouraged many people on their climb to success, and many of them are enjoying their well-deserved success. Throughout my career as a mental health official I have taught my clients the importance of self-esteem, of loving and appreciating themselves for who they are; that enables them to love and appreciate others (as we talked about in chapter 2). If it weren't for love in our lives, people would not be helping other people.

I believe the tyranny of hatred is being replaced by a loving consciousness.
—Wayne W. Dyer[28]

If each of us learns to love, praise, and appreciate ourselves and others, we can help make the world a better place to live.

Step: Thank and appreciate those who have helped you along your journey.

Tip: As we bless others, God blesses us, so it's a win-win situation. How can you go wrong?

---

28   Wayne W. Dyer, *There Is a Spiritual Solution to Every Problem* (New York: Harper, 2001), 163.

CHAPTER 13

Evidence of a Worthwhile Goal—My Invention

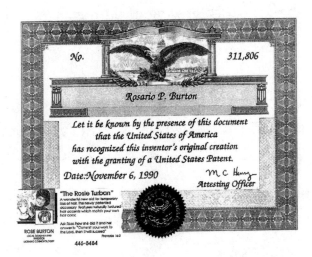

No. 311,806

Rosario P. Burton

Let it be known by the presence of this document
that the United States of America
has recognized this inventor's original creation
with the granting of a United States Patent.

Date: November 6, 1990

M C Henry
Attesting Officer

"The Rosie Turban"
A wonderful new aid for temporary
loss of hair. The newly patented
accessory features naturally textured
hair accents which match your own
hair color.

ROSE BURTON
LOCAL DESIGNER AND
INVENTOR
LICENSED COSMETOLOGIST

Ask Rose how she did it and her
answer is "Commit your work to
the Lord, then it will succeed."
Proverbs 16:3

446-8484

Because the Creator made me a creative person, I was able to create reality by inventing the Rosie Turban for cancer patients. I consider this my greatest contribution to humanity so far. Since God gave me the vision and inspiration, it is my greatest pleasure to give God all the glory.

Step: Give glory to where glory is due.

Tip: Look around you. Whether you're looking at individuals, properties, restaurants, resorts, or children's toys—whatever—ask yourself, what more would be helpful? What is needed? Developing such a mind-set opens your eyes. My cancer patients needed a way to cover their heads and feel attractive. Giving thought to their needs is what gave me the inspiration, desire, and creativity to invent the Rosie Turban. Give it a try; you may be very surprised at what you come up with.

CHAPTER 14

Fearless People Achieve Great Things

My first solo flight.

Fearless people seek adventure; they explore. They are high achievers whom nothing can stop. Some people possess

God-given powers to understand instructions. If that's correct, I must be one of those people because the instructions for learning to fly an airplane came very easy to me. I am thankful to God for that!

> *The Lord says, "I will guide you along*
> *the best pathway for your life.*
> *I will advise you and watch over you."*
> —Psalm 32:8 (NLT)

Flying is a way to appreciate and see all the natural beauty God created for us to enjoy. It's awesome!

I never dreamed about flying when I was young, but as I grew and learned the power of my mind and all the principles and steps I have discussed in this book, my confidence soared, and I did too! Yes, anyone can!

Step: Be patient but determined to work toward your success.

Tip: Always believe you can do it!

CHAPTER 15

The Power of Listening

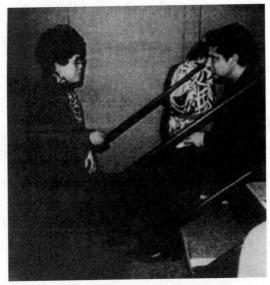

Dr. Deepak Chopra and Dr. Rose Burton

Dr. Deepak Chopra, an alternative medicine advocate, public speaker, writer, and physician known all over the world, is one of my favorite mentors because he knows how to create rapport and listen to others. As you can imagine from the picture above, he listened to me for a long time. He listens with great intensity; he lets the words and comments penetrate deep into his creative mind. The world needs more doctors like Dr. Chopra. We can all benefit greatly from studying and practicing his techniques.

Step: Listen intently to others.

Tip: For more helpful and enlightening information, check out Dr. Chopra's website: www.deepakchopra.com.

CHAPTER 16

The Power to Get In the Door

House Majority
TRUST

THE HOUSE MAJORITY TRUST
REQUESTS THE PRESENCE OF

Ms. Rosario Burton

*To attend and participate
In the Inauguration of*

George W. Bush
As President of the United States of America

and

Richard B. Cheney
As Vice President of the United States of America

On Thursday the twentieth of January
Two thousand and five
In the City of Washington, D.C.

In late 2004, I received a formal invitation to attend George W. Bush's presidential inauguration. It was my immense honor to attend this prestigious event. I was selected to attend due to my volunteer work and support for the Republican Party, outstanding leadership in business, and contributions to the local economy.

Who would have thought by volunteering my time that I would end up at the White House for the inauguration of a president? Phenomenal!

Step: Getting involved in volunteer work is very rewarding and will often provide you with the opportunity to meet people who can help you on your road to success.

Tip: Give of yourself in this life; you'll never know what door it will take you through.

CHAPTER 17

Imagination

Since I love classics, I was selected to be one of the judges to preside over the voting of a classic car competition in May 2010. This event took place at a golf course in Green Valley, California. It's always fun to see old cars restored to their original beauty. With great joy and the help of my imagination, I was able to select the classic car for first prize.

Imagination is more important than knowledge, for knowledge is limited.
—Albert Einstein[29]

---

[29] Albert Einstein, "The Albert Einstein Archives," n.d., www.albert-einstein.org/archives5.html, accessed February 16, 2015.

On March 12, 2015 permission was granted for the use of a quote by Albert Einstein from Barbara Wolff, Einstein Information Officer, from the Albert Einstein Archives, Hebrew University of Jerusalem, Israel. The quote, "Imagination is more important than knowledge, for knowledge is limited" (see chapter 17) stems from an interview published on October 26, 1929 in the *Saturday Evening Post*. George Sylvester Viereck, an American journalist of German descent, interviewed Einstein in Berlin. It is obvious that the authenticity of this statement depended on the interviewer's ability to understand and write exactly the interviewee said. The conversation was conducted in German. We do not know in which language the interviewer put down his notes. Viereck's capacity to decipher his own notes seems to have been inadequate, and he was notorious for his rather casual handling of those illegible notes and for filling in some gaps with his own words and ideas. The reliability of the article about Einstein is further undermined with by other facts.

According to Denis Brian, the Americanized German Viereck was known as a "big-name hunter" after "capturing" Kaiser Wilhelm II, Premier Georges Clemenceau of France, Henry Ford, Sigmund Freud, and George Bernard Shaw. Because of his desire to interview the great and because of his inordinate egotism, Freud accused him of having a "superman complex." Upton Sinclair referred to him as "a pompous liar and hypocrite," and George Bernard Shaw questioned his accuracy. So it is a legitimate question whether Einstein actually said what Viereck eventually

Step: Be creative and use your imagination. That will stimulate your mind.

Tip: No matter what you're involved in, use your imagination; you'll be amazed at the outcome.

---

published. We can neither verify nor deny it; he may have said it this way or with different words.

CHAPTER 18

Gardening Is Relaxing

Me in my garden

Probably the most important contribution we can make to improve our health is relaxing. One excellent example of relaxation is gardening, which can enhance our immune systems and help us cope with stress. I mentioned gardening in chapter 6, "Work Can Be Fun," as an example of turning work into pleasure.

Something about planting (no pun intended) yourself among the dirt and flowers takes away stress. Your mind wanders from stressful thoughts to the beauty of the plants and flowers. Moving about in the fresh air and sunshine is physiologically soothing, quiets your mind, and helps you unwind; it's a great way to promote your physical health. Improved health, happiness, and relaxation; what more can you ask for? An added bonus is the pride and achievement you'll feel as a result of your time in the garden. If you have never tried your hand at gardening, give it a try. I bet you'll find a new love.

Step: Find ways to relax along your journey.

Tip: In our fast-paced world, we simply need to find ways to relax. Find your way to relax and take the time to do it when you're feeling stressed or uncreative; it helps!

CHAPTER 19

The Power of Touch

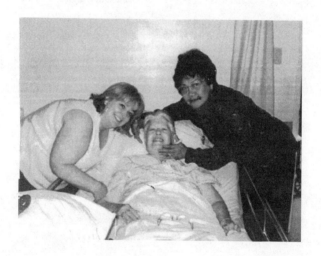

As I visited my cancer patient each day, I not only spoke with her, I also always gave her a loving touch. Patients are comforted by the knowledge that their doctors care. Touching is one of my powerful prescriptions, as you can see from this picture.

Touch is the first sense we acquire and one of the best means of encouraging communication and relaxation that soothes the immune system. Research shows that massage improves natural killer-cell activity, so let us consider touching as cognitive therapy.

Step: Give others loving touches; it's a form of communication.

Tip: Do you know someone who needs a hug today? That's something we can all do to comfort others.

CHAPTER 20

A Goal Reach

BUSINESS ADVISORY COUNCIL
National Republican Congressional Committee

For Immediate Release: Contact: NRCC Headquarters
December 20, 2006

*** DR. ROSARIO B. BURTON OF VACAVILLE
TO BE AWARDED
CONGRESSIONAL MEDAL OF DISTINCTION ***

WASHINGTON, DC - NRCC Chairman Tom Reynolds and the National Republican Congressional
Committee (NRCC) announced today that Dr. Rosario B. Burton has been chosen as a 2006
Congressional Medal of Distinction winner.

Dr. Burton was selected based on unyielding support of the Republican Party, outstanding leadership
in business and contributions to the local economy.

Only an elite group of business and professional people were nominated to receive the award before
the awards selection committee reached a final decision.

Commenting on Dr. Burton's selection, Congressman Reynolds said, "Dr. Burton has served as an
Honorary Chairman of the Business Advisory Council and has provided much needed support. This
award could not have gone to a more deserving candidate."

###

In 2006, I was once again fortunate to be invited to the White House while George W. Bush was serving as president. I was awarded the Congressional Medal of Distinction for outstanding leadership in business and contributions to the local economy for inventing the Rosie Turban (which I mentioned before). The ceremony took place in a beautiful room of the White House, and the medal I was awarded is stunning. As the medal was placed around my neck, I felt extremely honored. This was the peak of my goal reach; I was able to reach this goal, and you can do the same.

Step: Work hard and persevere.

Tip: You may not have a desire to invent something, but whatever your goal, don't stop until you reach your peak!

CHAPTER 21

Desire

Desire for something or to do something is where it all begins. What do you desire? Desire is a sense of longing or hoping for a person, object, or outcome; it's a "sense" each of us experiences often. It's the same sense or feeling expressed by our emotions, such as when we crave ice cream.

When you want to do something, accomplish something—a goal or a dream—your sense of longing, yearning, and craving is excited by the pleasurable thoughts and anticipation urging you to take action to accomplish whatever it is. Without the desire, you would have no motivation, hope, eagerness, or enthusiasm to move forward and accomplish your goal.

Aspire to something greater than yourself.
Develop a magnificent obsession.
—Dr. Dennis Kimbro and
Dr. Napoleon Hill[30]

Individuals with strong desires are often fearless and courageous and have the power to keep going regardless of obstacles. Have you ever met such a person? What is his or her secret? They use their desires to motivate themselves and others, take action, and overcome their problems. Dr. Dennis Kimbro and Napoleon Hill, authors of *Think and Grow Rich: A Black Choice*, stated, "Out of strong desire grow the motivating forces that cause men to embrace hopes, initiate plans, develop courage, and stimulate their minds to action in pursuit of a definite plan or purpose."[31]

From more that Dr. Kimbro had to say, I surmised that desire was an impulse we

---

[30] Kimbro and Hill, *Think and Grow Rich*, 3.
[31] Ibid., 71.

could transform into action. Also, if each of us can stimulate our own minds to produce this desire, we must also be capable of achieving that desire. I believe he is right on!

My intense desire to write this book helped me overcome the obstacles that came my way. I started with a positive attitude and was able to visualize beyond my obstacles. That increased my enthusiasm and motivated me to use all the techniques I have mentioned to achieve success.

Sometimes, we can get bogged down in the midst of our obstacles and forget the steps we have learned (knowledge) to move forward. Once I became aware I was stuck and not moving toward my goal, I took action utilizing all the techniques and steps to attain victory.

You can develop your desire by thinking about whatever you want to achieve. Once you've decided it's worth the effort and time, your desire will grow. Next, visualize your goal as though you have achieved it; don't allow negative thoughts to creep in. Visualization will definitely increase your desire.

Read everything you can pertaining to your goal to become knowledgeable about your subject. The more you know about it, the more exciting it becomes, and the more your desire grows. Talk with other people who are successes; as they reveal to you some of the techniques they used to achieve success, that will inspire you and your desire will grow.

Consider the benefits you stand to gain and how you'll feel once you reach your goal. Thinking about this will be so exciting that your desire will strengthen you more. Don't forget to repeat positive affirmations two or three times a day, and believe in what you're telling your creative self. Your desire is really up there, so no more procrastinating. You can do it! Think, believe, see, feel, and then claim your desire. Your desire will help you develop the courage to stimulate your mind to action. Yes, anyone can!

Here are some self-motivational materials I have found to be particularly helpful.

- The Bible, and I find a study Bible is easier to read and comprehend.

- *The Secret of the Ages* by Robert Collier contains basic ideas that opened up new vistas of living for countless people.
- *Think and Grow Rich* by Napoleon Hill is a must-read for anyone wanting to improve his or her life and think positively.

Robert Collier said, "Unless you want a certain thing 'in the worst way' and manifest that desire in the shape of a strong, impelling force, you will have no will with which to accomplish anything."[32] Dr. Collier thinks that we must firmly want to do something or possess something to arouse ourselves to a state of insatiable desire. By doing so, we will set in motion one of nature's most powerful mental forces.

The starting point of all achievement is desire.
—Napoleon Hill[33]

---

[32] Kimbro and Hill, *Think and Grow Rich*, 80.
[33] Ibid.

Step: Plant a strong, unquenchable desire in your mind.

Tip: By thinking in a positive way, you can claim the desire, which is the starting point of all achievement.

CHAPTER 22

Lifelong Lessons

Our experiences and the lessons we have learned shape us. Life is a lesson regardless of where or when we learn it. Growing up, graduating from high school, going to college, starting our first job, buying our first car and first home, getting married, raising kids—these are all opportunities and learning experiences. We may view them as memorable experiences or struggles; it all depends on how we look at life—positively or negatively or perhaps not caring either way.

Used positively, each event in our lives can be an enriching lesson. We can look at it positively and score an A or look at it negatively and score a D; the choice is ours. If we live life with all the gusto we can muster up and have faith, we'll experience joy and happiness. We will encounter struggles, but a positive outlook will get us through them much better, and we will learn valuable lessons along the way.

We're more likely to succeed if we have a positive attitude. Opportunities are all around us; we just need to decide what and how much we want to accomplish. This action is a goal reach. Reaching your goals is what you want to do, right? Yes, it does take effort, determination, and persistence, but the payoff is so worth it.

You might be thinking, *Easy for you to say. You're a doctor.* Well, I haven't always been a doctor, and I've had to endure many struggles. Fortunately, I learned to think positively very early in life and grew from all my experiences. C. S. Lewis said, "You are never too old to set another goal or to dream a new dream."[34] He was so right, and

---

[34] C. S. Lewis (1898–1963); novelist, poet, academic, medievalist, literary critic, essayist, lay theologian, broadcaster, lecturer, and Christian apologist.

I'm proof of that. I've lived a long life and have found success I'm most grateful for, but I haven't stopped, and I have no plans to. I am determined, and you can be too!

A beautician had a client who was a doctor. One day, while the beautician was working on her hair, the doctor said, "One of the nicest things I enjoy about you is your ability to listen. Why don't you go to night school to become a licensed mental health official?" The beautician knew that would be difficult and a real challenge; it would mean she would have to work all day and attend school at night and then find time to do homework, but she took the doctor's advice, attended night school, and became a licensed mental health official. It was difficult, no doubt about it, but the payoff was worth it. From that time on, her life was changed for the better.

The mental health official happens to be me, and I hope my story will inspire you to persevere and accomplish all your heart's desires. I use my personal experiences and accomplishments in this book for motivation and educational purposes.

Step: Learn to find the good in all circumstances in life.

Tip: As you go through life and encounter good as well as bad, remember to always make the choice to look at the positive side of your situation.

CHAPTER 23

Believing in Yourself and Avoiding Inferiority

Eleanor Roosevelt said, "No one can make you feel inferior without your consent."[35] But how can we avoid feeling inferior? First, we must love and honor ourselves as I discussed in chapter 2, Love and Kindness. Mrs. Roosevelt was so correct in her statement because giving our consent to agree or not is a choice we can make. We must not let anyone's opinion affect our positive self-image; we must always believe we are important and valuable.

---

[35] Eleanor Roosevelt, an American politician and the longest-serving first lady of the United States.

So if we are valuable, how much is our worth? In *Think and Grow Rich: A Black Choice*, Dr. Kimbro stated,

> Researchers now know that there is an electronic energy of hydrogen atoms in the human body. They calculated that if this electronic energy of the hydrogen atoms in the human body could be utilized, a single person could supply the electricity of a large highly industrialized country for nearly a week.[36]

Dr. Kimbro believes the atoms in our bodies contain a potential energy charge of more than 11 million kilowatt-hours per pound. So, it's estimated that the average person is worth about $85 billion. Our electrons and atoms are not just particles or matter but actual waves of living energy. These waves flow out of us and spread themselves in forms that reflect and

---

[36] Kimbro and Hill, *Think and Grow Rich*, 146.

move but are undetectable by our eyes. Fascinating, isn't it? It sounds as though we could all become super wealthy if we could harness this personal energy. Maybe that should be one of our goals—"How to Harness Our Personal Hydrogen Atoms"!

All kidding aside, how can we avoid or get free from feelings of inferiority? Throughout this book, I have written about the importance of a positive attitude and self-image. Without these qualities, we can find it difficult to get motivated and achieve success.

If you're feeling inferior in any area of your life, pay close attention to the rest of this chapter. I hope it will open your eyes to a new reality. An inferiority complex is the sense of feeling lesser than others in some way or another. An inferiority complex is often an advanced state of discouragement, a feeling that everyone is better than you, a feeling of low self-worth and esteem. A superiority complex is of course the opposite; that can make people arrogant and stubborn. The ideal here is achieving a balance; a touch of an inferiority complex can makes us disciplined and determined, and a small amount of a superiority complex can give us self-confidence and strength.

Whenever you feel inadequate or insignificant, that's the time to focus on your positive qualities; think about what you enjoy doing. More than likely, you're very good at things you like doing. Write down your strengths; that act will help you build up your self-esteem. Think about all your achievements to date, the positives you have brought into your life. Ignore your failures; they just aren't that important. Remind yourself of all your worth. Anytime you start having belittling thoughts about yourself, stop them in their tracks!

The idea here is to train your mind to think positively about yourself. In time, you'll start feeling that you have value. God gave each of us uniqueness; that makes each of us very special. How could we not be if God made us? We aren't supposed to be like other people; God made us distinct with our own gifts and talents. Consider this when you start feeling down: God made you to be you, no one else. Once you begin to realize and believe this, you will look at yourself in a much brighter light.

As you walk on your journey, avoid people or places that make you feel inferior. Why set yourself up for feeling bad about yourself? Take all opportunities to surround yourself with people who love and appreciate you; that will be a super boost for your morale. But you can't always be around people who love and accept you; there will be times when you just have to go along to get along. The important thing is stay positive no matter what.

Another part of this process is taking care of yourself physically and emotionally, which I covered earlier. Nutrition, exercise, and rest are important. When you take care of yourself, pamper yourself, and have some fun, you will feel good about yourself, and that will boost your positive self-image. You will be able to recognize the good things that happen to you. When you acknowledge your blessings, your load will become lighter just as your mood will become lighter. Don't you love it when a smile comes to your face automatically or when you laugh aloud about something? That can start happening more and more as your positive self-image increases. Nice thought, huh? It can happen!

Because the process is slow, we sometimes don't realize the changes taking place in us. It won't happen overnight, so we should give ourselves time—we should be patient and stay at it. One day, we will wake up and notice the new us.

Step: Let go of all negative feelings and build a positive self-image.

Tip: Building a positive self-image will make life happier for those around you as well as yourself.

CHAPTER 24

Powerful Affirmations for Success

Positive self-affirmation is an excellent aid in achieving success. If you want to be successful, you have to identify, affirm, and expect success. In *This Thing Called You*, Dr. Ernest Holmes suggested that we must employ powerful affirmations such as the examples below.

- I expect everything I do to prosper.
- I enthusiastically expect success.
- I let good flow into my experiences.
- I am seeing good in every direction I look.
- I am looking forward to more good.

- I am entering into a deeper understanding of life.
- I am recognizing my union with all people and all events.[37]

Why is it so necessary to identify and affirm to be successful? Dr. Holmes wrote, "It is because the law of identity is a definite thing … That with which you mentally identify yourself sets up an image of thought in your consciousness which tends to attract the situations with which you are mentally identified."[38] That means our entire unconscious thoughts continually engage or resist.

We can use powerful affirmations by controlling our mental reactions so that they will automatically become affirmative. We will learn how to utilize our creative minds and identify and believe in what and how much we want to have. Some experts call this process the laboratory of the mind. When you master this technique, you will have an abundance of what you want.

---

[37] Holmes, *This Thing Called You*, 63.
[38] Ibid., 62–63.

Once you know what your goal is, identify creative and appropriate affirmations that will assist you on your journey to success.

Step: Master your affirmations.

Tip: You must visualize your desire, expect it, and claim it as though it is already a reality.

CHAPTER 25

If You Really Want to Make Great Things Happen, You Can!

Photographer: Jen Bougher

The following action words can make things happen.

Act   Affirm

Aspire	Formulate
Believe	Hope
Claim	Imagine
Desire	Inspire
Dream	Invent
Expect	Think
Feel	

These words also represent the unlimited power within you that will program your mind for success.

I used a picture of a rose because they were considered the most sacred flower in ancient Egypt. Many individuals have searched for their fragrance, and so it is with the fragrance of success. Find your personal fragrance.

Step: Follow the action words at the beginning of this chapter.

Tip: The more you engage the action words, the better your success will be.

CHAPTER 26

Less Negative Stress

We all have the so-called hidden stressors in life. Dr. Hans Selye, a scientist, author and ten-times winner of the Nobel Prize, is known as the father of stress. He wrote, "Stress is the nonspecific response of the body to any demand, whether it is caused by, or results in, pleasant or unpleasant conditions."[39] He points out that stress is not always a negative occurrence; it can frequently come from joyous and pleasurable experiences as well.

But how can we fight negative stress? In chapter 18, I pointed out that gardening

---

[39]   Dr. Hans Selye, a scientist, author and ten-time Nobel prize winner known as the "father of stress."

is a wonderful way I relieve my negative stress. When I work in the garden, I focus on beautiful plants and flowers, and I find that calming and restful; it creates a radiant feeling that words cannot describe.

Give gardening a try. I'm sure you will relax, and that will allow your creative mental juices to flow. Without realizing it, your body and mind will shed negative stress and achieve a level of tranquility. Don't you feel relaxed already? Trust me. You'll enjoy gardening and the benefits it brings.

If gardening isn't your thing, choose other ways to fight stress that include affirmation, exercise, meditation, and prayer. I realize you are different from everyone else and require different techniques to find peace and calm. If you have tried other options of achieving tranquility but haven't yet achieved it, consider talking about it with a friend or perhaps a professional.

Step: Relieve all negative stress.

Tip: If you haven't tried gardening yet, do so. It can heal your body and soul.

CHAPTER 27

Don't Quit

When things go wrong—and they will at times—don't quit. We all have experienced what we call failure and have been tempted to give up at times. But that will not allow us to achieve success.

We should all consider our failures as learning experiences. We can learn from our mistakes if we are willing to. If our plan A doesn't work, we should move on to plan B—a new action may result in a new result. We will find it impossible to succeed if we give up.

Here are some details about someone who failed repeatedly but never gave up.

- He failed in his business at age twenty-one.
- He was defeated when he ran for legislature at age twenty-two.
- He failed again in business at age twenty-four.
- His sweetheart died when he was twenty-six.
- He had a nervous breakdown at age twenty-seven.
- He again lost a congressional race at age thirty-six.
- He lost a senatorial race at age forty-five.
- He lost the race of vice president at age forty-seven.
- He again lost a senatorial race at age forty-nine.
- At age fifty-two, he was elected president of the United States.

This courageous man was Abraham Lincoln, our sixteenth president. How did he do it in spite of all his setbacks? His attitude was positive, and he refused to quit. His vision was of victory.

One person took the California bar exam twenty-five times before he passed it at age forty-seven. "Don't give up," Maxcy Filer, councilman and lawyer says. When someone asked him why he had continued to try so hard, he said, "I don't quit … I look at it from the standpoint that the bar exam was passable for others and so it shall be for me. I believe in sticking to it and keep going. If I can do it, you can too!"[40]

Step: Never give up. Never quit.

Tip: Remember these three words that apply to Maxcy Filer: perseverance, perseverance, perseverance.

---

[40] Cynthia Kersey, *Unstoppable*, 279–81.

CHAPTER 28

Super Achiever

With a healthy mind and body, anyone can be a super achiever. What are the requirements for becoming a super achiever? They are simple and natural. If we think about how people progress, grow, learn, and so on from the time they're born, we're on the road (without even realizing it) to becoming achievers. The "super" part comes in with how enthusiastic we become in achieving. Infants learn that if they cry, they will receive attention; achievement number one. Babies learn if they move their arms and legs, they can crawl to get somewhere: achievement number two. When toddlers start walking, they become "super" at moving around: achievement number three. Even when they fall, they learn they can get up.

And so it is with life at any age; we learn we can get up, and that's the key to becoming super achievers—not giving up. One step at a time, we gain confidence, go for it, and achieve. When we realize we can achieve, we want to achieve even more. Just like those little guys who went from crying to crawling and then to walking, running, and jumping, we can develop and master our abilities.

We must never stop. We should all do what we're capable of doing and then some. We will all start by taking baby steps, so learn a lesson from toddlers and never give up. If someone else has succeeded at what you're trying to accomplish, then you can too. Just remember the visualization skills I mentioned. As you achieve something, your confidence level will increase, and that will give you the mental stamina to achieve even more.

Dr. Robert Schuller believes that "power" words can motivate us. He developed a helpful formula.

I am = I can
I—I am = I can
C—Curiosity builds confidence
A—Anything is possible
N—Never give up[41]

On *Dancing with the Stars*, one of the contestants was a beautiful woman with a disability. According to the announcer, she had lost her feet due to an illness, but with the aid of two artificial feet, she danced gracefully and won a prize. Her secret was that she didn't allow herself to give up; even with her disability, she found a way. If she could do it, we can too! Her belief, positive attitude, determination, and perseverance brought her victory. By believing, affirming, and visualizing, we too can have that "I can do it" attitude. It takes practice and patience, but it will pay off, and we will have

---

[41]   Dr. Robert Schuller, *Power Thoughts: Achieve Your True Potential through Power Thinking* (New York: Harpercollins, 1993), 194.

a better chance of accomplishing our goals much sooner and better than we expected.

Step: Begin with belief and visualization.

Tip: Unless you start, you will never finish.

CHAPTER 29

The Decision Is Yours

The previous chapters contain advice that can help you accomplish great things. I hope you have learned to program your mind to achieve whatever your heart desires. But it all relies on your starting toward your goal and not giving up; you can do this by utilizing all the principles and techniques I've covered. No one can think or do it for you; you must make your decisions yourself for your life.

You must be ready and willing to move forward and act upon the realistic decisions you make. Study the life stories of great men and women who from humble beginnings cleared the obstructions they came across and achieved success.

If you follow the principles and techniques I've laid out in this book and combine those with determination and persistence, you will achieve victory.

> *Men talk as if victory were something fortunate. Work is victory.*
> —Ralph Waldo Emerson[42]

Start working right now and you'll get to your destination; time waits for no one. Each day that passes is a day no more. Get started on the desires of your heart and create your new beginnings to achieve life's best. Whatever you do, make it a labor of love with a grateful and positive attitude.

Love one another, be kind to one another, and give of yourself as often as possible.

---

[42] Ralph Waldo Emerson (1803–1882).

Those who possess "agape love"
are the happiest individuals on earth
because their love is authentic.
Dr. Rose P. Burton, author
of *Yes—Anyone Can!*

Step: Make decisions for your life.

Tip: The decision is yours, so make it!

CHAPTER 30

How to Find Success

If you practice seeing yourself in your mind's eye doing or creating what you really want, it will enhance your success and nothing will be able to stop you from becoming the person you believe you are.

Set your goals, and decide what you want. What is your heart's desire to accomplish? Develop a plan, do not procrastinate, and take action. You're on the mark. Ready, set, go!

While working on your goal, review and apply as often as needed the following positive, dynamic, and creative thinking principles covered in this book.

1. Desire
2. Imagination
3. Faith
4. Positive Self-Image
5. Positive Mental Attitude
6. Enthusiasm
7. Belief
8. Perseverance
9. Mind Programming
10. Visualization
11. Affirmations
12. Expecting and Accepting
13. Giving to Others
14. Self-Discipline
15. Don't Quit

If you truly use all the principles, techniques, and steps in this book, great things will happen to you, and your life will never be the same; it will forever be better! As a result, you'll discover what you are looking for. Yes, anyone can!

Remember that you have been given the secrets to attracting success by using the Three Big C Principles: our heavenly Creator created you to be a creator filled with Creativeness, so you can Create anything. Go forth and create your lifelong goals and dreams, and as you learn and grow, pay it forward by helping others learn to do the same. In so doing, you will benefit all humanity.

Thank you for reading my book. My hope is that it has opened your eyes to new possibilities and given you encouragement and enthusiasm to move forward in a positive direction in life. It is also my heart's desire that you are the recipient of a wonderful, joyous, loving life filled with great belief and great success.

I wish you all God's blessings.

—Dr. Rose P. Burton

FINAL THOUGHT

When I reflect on my life and accomplishments, I see God's hand in it. Some things I asked Him for while others He knew I needed to learn and grow in. He provided me an abundance of people and circumstances to help me succeed in the areas of my desires and His will for me. I give Him all the glory in all I do, but I'm not done yet. I still have goals to achieve, and I know He is beside me all the way.

FINAL SELF-INSTRUCTION

*There is just one life for
each of us: our own.*
Euripides[43]

Take a few seconds and think, see, and feel
with intensity. Tell yourself, *I have already
achieved all that I want to possess in life.*
Thinking it, saying it, and feeling it will make
it reality.

---

[43]   Euripides, c. 480–406 BC, Greek poet.

ABOUT THE AUTHOR

Dr. Rose P. Burton is a licensed retired mental health official. She earned graduate degrees in clinical psychology from Southern California University for professional studies and obtained a degree as a doctoral addiction counselor. She is an active member of the National Board of Addiction Examiners.

Dr. Burton is also an honorary member of the Cambridge *Who's Who* registry of executives and professionals and is the inventor of the Rosie Turban for cancer patients (Patent 311806).

Dr. Burton said the people in her life that influenced her the most are Dr. Pilar Avedilio, a physician in charge of the City

Health Center in Zamboanga City in the Philippines. Dr. Avedilio was her model of excellence who assisted her in turning her dreams into reality. Dr. Avedilio was also the first person to teach Dr. Burton to never quit.

Once Dr. Burton stepped on American soil, she met another person who influenced her life greatly, Dr. Nelson, who awakened Dr. Burton to her unlimited abilities and discovery of her road map to success. Dr. Nelson encouraged Dr. Burton to further her education, which in turn became a great opportunity for Dr. Burton to grow emotionally, socially, physiologically, and most of all spiritually.

Dr. Burton gives credit to Abraham Lincoln, someone who despite the failures he encountered never gave up.

Dr. Burton believes that if people don't have others in their lives who can help them, reading about the lives of those who have succeeded can be of tremendous assistance in personal development.

Dr. Burton wrote this book because she believes that we should continually pass on the good fortune that has come our way to others. In this way, we can pass on our individual legacies to generations to come.

NOTES

Chapter 1
Merriam-Webster online Dictionary, www.merriam-webster.
  com/dictionary/success.

Chapter 2
Merriam-Webster online Dictionary, www.merriam-webster.
  com/dictionary/kindness.
Mother Teresa "Mother Teresa of Calcutta Center," n.d.,
  www.motherteresa.org/layout.html, accessed February
  19, 2015.
Dr. Richard Carlson, *Don't Worry, Make Money: Spiritual &*
  Practical Ways to Create Abundance and More Fun in
  Your Life (New York: Hyperson, 1997), 148

Chapter 3
Iyanla Vanzant, *The Spirit of A Man: A Vision of Transformation*
  for Black Men and the Women Who Love Them (San
  Francisco: HarperOne 1997), 185.
Dr. Norman Vincent Peale, *Enthusiasm Makes the Difference*
  (New York: Touchstone, 2003), 4, 12, 129, 130.

Chapter 4

Merriam-Webster online Dictionary, www.merriam-webster.com/dictionary/happiness.

Dr. Martin E. P. Seligman, *Authentic Happiness: Using the New Positive Psychology to Realize Your Potential for Lasting Fulfillment* (New York: Atria Books, 2004), 44–45.

A. R. Bernard, *Happiness Is … Simple Steps to a Life of Joy* (New York: Touchstone, 2011), 11, 160, quote by Dr. Robert Schuller.

Chapter 5

Ann Hibbard, "Treasured Friends: Finding and Keeping True Friendships," n.d.

www.christianbookpreviews.com/christian-book-excerpt.php?isbn=0800787137, accessed February 19, 2015.

Aristotle.

Ralph Waldo Emerson (1803–1882).

Chapter 6

Dennis Kimbro and Napoleon Hill, *Think and Grow Rich: A Black Choice* (New York: Fawcet, 1991), 37.

Johann Wolfgang Von Goethe (1749–1832).

Chapter 9

William Whewell (1794–1866). One of the most influential figures in nineteenth-century Britain. Whewell was an extensive writer on many subjects.

Confucius (551–479 BC).

Dennis Kimbro and Napoleon Hill, *Think and Grow Rich: A Black Choice* (New York: Fawcet, 1991), 87.

Chapter 10

Dr. Ernest Holmes, *This Thing Called You* (New York: BN Publishing, 2007), 18.

Cynthia Kersey, *Unstoppable* (Naperville, IL Sourcebooks, 1998), 127, quote by Muhammad Ali.

Dennis Kimbro and Napoleon Hill, *Think and Grow Rich: A Black Choice* (New York: Fawcet, 1991), 49.

Chapter 11

Claude M. Bristol, *The Magic of Believing* (Chicago: Snowball Publishing, 2011), 1.

Dr. E. Carol Webster, *Success Management: How to get to the Top and Keep Your Sanity Once You Get There* (Florida: Privileged Communications, 1993), 2 of acknowledgements.

Dr. William James, "QuoteWorld," www.quoteworld.org/quotes/7110, accessed February 16, 2015.

Josephine Carlton, *Life Messages: Inspiration for the Woman's Spirit* (New Jersey: Andrews McMeel Publishing, 2002), 171, quote from Dr. Nancy J. Currie.

Genesis 1:31 NLT.

Chapter 12

Dr. Robert Schuller, *Power Thoughts: Achieve Your True Potential through Power Thinking* (New York: Harpercollins, 1993), 236.

Patsy Clairmont et al., *Laughter Is the Spice of Life* (Tennessee: W Publishing, 2004), 176, quote by Benjamin Franklin.

Wayne W. Dyer, *There is a Spiritual Solution to Every Problem* (New York: Harper, 2001), 163.

Chapter 17

Albert Einstein, "The Albert Einstein Archives," www.albert-einstein.org/archives5.html, accessed February 16, 2015.

Chapter 21

Dennis Kimbro and Napoleon Hill, *Think and Grow Rich: A Black Choice* (New York: Fawcet, 1991), 3, 71, 80, quote from Robert Collier.

Napoleon Hill, *Think and Grow Rich* (CreateSpace Independent Publishing, 2010).

Chapter 22

C. S. Lewis (1898–1963), a novelist, poet, academic, medievalist, literary critic, essayist, lay theologian, broadcaster, lecturer, and Christian apologist.

Chapter 23

Dennis Kimbro and Napoleon Hill, *Think and Grow Rich: A Black Choice* (New York: Fawcet, 1991), 146.

Chapter 24

Dr. Ernest Holmes, *This Thing Called You* (New York: BN Publishing, 2007), 62–63.

Chapter 26

Dr. Hans Selya, a scientist, author and ten-times Nobel prize winner known as the father of stress.

Chapter 27

Abraham Lincoln (1809–1865), the sixteenth president of the United States.

Cynthia Kersey, *Unstoppable* (Naperville, IL: Sourcebooks, 1998), 279–81.

Chapter 28

Dr. Robert Schuller, *Power Thoughts: Achieve Your True Potential through Power Thinking* (New York: Harpercollins, 1993), 194.

Chapter 29

Ralph Waldo Emerson (1803–1882).

Final Self-Instruction

Euripides (c. 480–406 BC), Greek poet.

Printed in the United States
By Bookmasters